Creating Fantastic Vases

Creating Fantastic Vases

50 Fun & Fabulous Ideas & Projects

Suzanne J. E. Tourtillott

LARK BOOKS

A Division of Sterling Publishing Co., Inc.
New York

Editor: Suzanne J. E. Tourtillott
Art Director: Tom Metcalf
Assistant Art Director: Shannon Yokeley
Photographer: Keith Wright Photography
Cover Designer: Barbara Zaretsky
Illustrator: Orrin Lundgren
Production Assistance: Avery Johnson
Editorial Assistance: Delores Gosnell, Veronika Alice Gunter,
Anne Wolff Hollyfield, Rain Newcomb

Library of Congress Cataloging-in-Publication Data

Creating fantastic vases : 50 fun & fabulous ideas & projects / Suzanne
J. E. Tourtillott, editor.-- 1st ed.
    p. cm.
  ISBN 1-57990-407-6
  1. Vases. I. Tourtillott, Suzanne J. E.
  TT899.6.C74 2003
  745.593--dc21

10 9 8 7 6 5 4 3 2 1

First Edition

Published by Lark Books, a division of
Sterling Publishing Co., Inc.
387 Park Avenue South, New York, N.Y. 10016

© 2003, Lark Books

Distributed in Canada by Sterling Publishing,
c/o Canadian Manda Group, One Atlantic Ave., Suite 105
Toronto, Ontario, Canada M6K 3E7

Distributed in the U.K. by Guild of Master Craftsman Publications Ltd.
Castle Place, 166 High Street, Lewes, East Sussex, England BN7 1XU
Tel: (+ 44) 1273 477374, Fax: (+ 44) 1273 478606
Email: pubs@thegmcgroup.com, Web: www.gmcpublications.com

Distributed in Australia by Capricorn Link (Australia) Pty Ltd.
P.O. Box 704, Windsor, NSW 2756 Australia

If you have questions or comments about this book, please contact:
Lark Books
67 Broadway
Asheville, NC 28801
(828) 253-0467

Manufactured In China

ISBN 1-57990-407-6

contents

The Perfect Pair

The moment I've cut a flower or stem from the earth, I'm determined to keep its vibrant, wordless presence with me as long as is humanly possible. During the days or even weeks ahead, these silent houseguests will deliver many moments of gladness, and I will glory in them.

I've discovered that this pleasure can be enhanced by the kind of vase the flowers are placed in. Each pairing can be a celebration, however brief. And although you may have an array of perfectly acceptable flower containers, perhaps you've wondered, as I have, how they might better do justice to nature's beauty.

Creating Fantastic Vases offers 50 distinctive flower containers that show you how to combine an exquisite vase with your glorious cuttings; plus they make marvelous home accessories. You can start with whatever's at hand: some of these amazing vases began as plain ordinary store-boughts or flea-market finds; others were made from scratch with beautiful, yet unexpected, materials. In all cases, the talented designers show you how to create vases as memorable as the flowers themselves.

6

Vases for All Time

Vases—those divine objects that are both artful and useful— long ago captured our collective imagination. Humbly useful, loved for their inspired decorative motifs, vases have somehow survived war, pestilence, and even the occasional household disaster. Indeed, vessels throughout the ages can be appreciated as cultural icons that represent ideals of design and function. Squat or skinny, ceramic or glass, vases are some of the most endearing and lasting artifacts we possess.

Although the creation of the first vases was surely inspired by need, the possibilities of form soon equaled that of function. Long before the potter's wheel was invented (as long as 10,000 years ago), clay vases were shaped by hand. The animated silhouettes of everyday scenes on a Greek Attic vase moved John Keats to praise its enduring and timeless symbolism. When you think about it, any vase you might own or admire today is, in some fashion, an ode to this ancient form.

In their shape and decoration, vases inspired great art around the world. Arabian pots, with their turquoise colors and floral arabesque designs, may well have reached their artistic height some 35

centuries ago. They're often considered among the most beautiful in the world. No less fascinating are the spouted sculptural forms of 2,200-year-old Peruvian clay containers, stirrup-handled for easier transportation. Their surfaces abound with lively images of priests, soldiers, working men and women, faces, cats, birds, and snakes. Across the ocean at around this same time, women from African tribal societies were making round, flare-necked pots, decorated with geometric patterns and silhouettes of people, to keep foods cool in the desert. In 100 CE, Pueblo Indians of the American Southwest and Mixtecs, natives of Central America, began putting legs on their vases, most likely to keep their contents away from vermin, but this functional component also increased their aesthetic appeal.

China's delicately polychromed enamel-and-gold Qing dynasty porcelains have been prized for generations the world over. They, in turn, inspired the fabulous pedestal vases with finely tooled gilt work from the great continental and English porcelain houses of the 18th and 19th centuries. The Japanese looked to China as well for inspiration for their vase production

Liz Quackenbush. *Dolphin Pocket Vase*. 1992. 14 x 9 x 7 inches (35.6 x 22.9 x 17.8 cm). Hand-built terra cotta; maiolica; gold lustre

before developing unique *ikebana* container styles seven centuries ago. These flat, tall, or freestyle vases are still used for simple, but striking, flower arrangements.

In Europe, Northern Renaissance painters depicted both stone and crystal vases in their beautiful flower portraits. These paintings reflect not only the artist's aesthetic interest in the vase, but also that of a rising middle class able to more easily acquire all sorts of well-crafted objects for home decoration, thereby fuelling a greater demand for decorative, yet functional, objects.

Today, contemporary vase styles compete with the valued ancients for our affection. Collectible designs sometimes are prized nearly as much for their quirky shapes and subject matter as for their true aesthetic form. Louis Tiffany's sinuous, sculptural Art Nouveau glass pieces are striking abstracts of natural forms. Vases in the Art Deco style (a movement that began in France in the early 1920s) were inspired by the influence of new machinery and mass production materials, using geometric shapes and strong color. Novelty head vases of beautiful women, made in the mid-20th century, are sought-after collectibles, and multihued cornucopia Arts and Crafts vases charm us as vivid reminders of a bygone era.

It seems that every vase converses with the past, whether we realize it or not. Those devised for specific

types of flowers, such as the 1930s-era lidded, pressed-glass rose bowls, or the extravagant, towering *tulipieres* that first appeared during the 17th-century tulip craze, are now appreciated not only for their beauty, but also for their evocation of an entire culture. It's still much as Keats expressed in his *Ode on a Grecian Urn:*

> What leaf-fring'd legend haunts about thy shape
> Of deities or mortals, or of both...
> **— John Keats (1795–1821)**

Form, Color, Contrast

The design fundamentals of shape, color, and contrast are the tools of the artist. Here's how to use them in your creative pursuit of the artful vase...even if you never put a single flower in it.

A narrow cylinder has a clean, contemporary look. Use strong, sturdy stems that match the lines of the vase. Extend the line of the container with a few dramatic blooms, or let an arrangement break free of its bonds by pairing the flowers with long, bare wood branches. The bud vase is important to a basic vase collection, too. Diminutive enough to keep a single rose stem from wavering, it looks satisfyingly full with only a few blossoms.

Square vases multitask well. Open up an arrangement with flowering branches or sturdy vines that curve and bend (but avoid just a few stems of flowers, which look skimpy and tilt to one side). For a closed look, pack the vase with bundles of slender twigs or grasses. Cylinders and squares are likely to require marbles, rocks, or some other form of frog to hold the flowers in place. Read more about frogs on page 11.

Play up the shape of the classic round vase with a narrow neck. Its flared body lets stems spread out generously from the narrower opening. Adjust the stem length to use more of the wide middle of the vase, and you'll achieve a dramatic fan-shape with them. You also can use pom-pom blooms, or create a globe-shape mixed bouquet to echo the basic vase shape.

A trumpet vase can hold an abundant armful that emphasizes its flaring neckline. Some trumpets have feet or stands for greater stability. A flower market bucket's modified trumpet shape widens slightly from the base, and has a casual look that's perfect for outdoor settings.

With a free-form or unconventional vase, you approach the challenge of decorating and arranging with a new spirit every time. If a pail, low bowl, or unusual planter shape doesn't control the direction of the stem enough, use one of the many methods described on pages 11—12 to do so.

No matter which shape you choose, size and proportion really matter. Use a vase roomy-enough to create elegant, spare arrangements with a single bloom or several, and let the negative space between and around them speak volumes. Or get the look of a lush, full mass by tying same-length stems of all-alike flowers into a bundle, so that the flower heads crowd together.

Color is important because it has emotional—even passionate—appeal, and there's no better way to describe a feeling response to color than to name its temperature, whether it's warm or cool. The interaction of hues actually influence our visual and emotional perceptions of them. You can use these basic color relationships to help you decorate a vase as well as choose your arrangement's colors—but be open to your own creative flair, too.

Set a theme, establish a mood, or celebrate a season with a color scheme. Harmonious groups use tints and shades of a single color. The effect of such a group in, say, lavender, violet, and blue-violet, is a restrained, cool color statement. Complementary pairs, such as orange and blue, or yellow and violet, are visually exciting opposites. These pairs have a natural affinity, but don't be constrained by them...your red-green pair might use deep pink and lime green. Elegant and timeless neutrals (white, black, grays, and browns) are easily spiced up with complementary colors. Bright, rainbow-hued color collections signify the festive height of summer.

Experiment, too, with the power of contrasts. Textures and materials very unlike each other will be somewhat muted with a harmonious treatment, while strong differences of light and dark make an emphatic graphic statement. Color also has visual weight. Dark colors seem to be heavier than pastels, but those similar in value (that is, their relative lightness or darkness) will appear to be more or less equal in weight.

Keep in mind that light is interactive. Just as the quality of light can be hazy and soft or brightly sparkling, color's impact changes in response to it; a low light level quiets color, while clear, direct light animates it. With transparent containers, the water itself is a design element that refracts and magnifies light rays. According to the principles of ikebana, a flower arrangement should be thought of as having three interrelated parts: the area under water, the area between the water line and the top of the container, and the space outside the top of the container. Naturally, these should have a pleasing and harmonious balance.

Essentials: Tools & Tips

You might expect the vase to do all the work, but the florist's kit of tools and tips makes it easier to get the look you want and also to treat your flowers with care.

A flower stem is full of vessels, much like our veins, that carry water and nutrients to all parts of the flower. If you expect them to have a long flower life, fresh-cut flowers on the porch, deck, or indoors need water, shade, and nourishment. Pick the freshest flowers, with healthy buds and leaves, and use a clean vase. Use floral pruners, light clippers, or scissors to cut green stems, and heavier florist's shears for woody or thick ones. Remove an inch (2.5 cm) or so from the purchased plant material when you get home. Make a diagonal cut, so the stem will rest on the point, leaving room for the water to flow into it. Remove bruised leaves, foliage, and stems from below the water line, or they'll quickly spoil the water. Before arranging cut flowers, condition the stems by floating them in warm water in a dark, cool place for several hours, or overnight. They need a big drink so the blooms will live as long as possible. Plucking flower buds as they begin to die prevents the other flowers from aging, too. Once the blooms begin to wilt, salvage them for another few days by cutting the stems again.

Dirty containers cause flowers to die quickly and can even pass on bacteria to other arrangements, so keep your vases clean between uses (try a bottlebrush on narrow ones). Wash sturdy, nonporous containers with warm soapy water, and rinse them with a weak bleach-and-water solution. Rinse the vase well with fresh water, and dry it thoroughly before storing it.

A frog, of course, is happy in or out of water, and florist's frogs must be just as versatile because they're used to arrange and hold all kinds of stems. A frog can be almost anything at all, from a pin-sharp metal holder (in the Japanese ikebana tradition) or a perforated glass half-sphere to cranberries or short lengths of bamboo. Antique flower frogs made from hand-blown glass or ornately twisted metal—usually rusted—are even prized as collectibles.

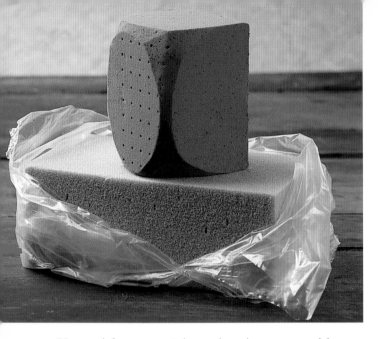

Unusual frog materials, such as lemons, marbles, or standing twigs, not only do the job, they become a beautiful part of the whole when used in a transparent vase.

Most likely you'll use an ordinary, inexpensive frog made·of foam, a loose ball of chicken wire, or even a simple grid of florist's tape over the vase's mouth. There are two basic types of floral foam,

dry and wet, available in various shapes, styles, textures, and sizes. Dry polystyrene block foam (the gray foam pictured above) is great for dried- and silk-flower arrangements. Simply cut the block with a knife so it fits inside the container, and put the stems in it. Wet floral foam is soft and highly absorbent, but use it only once because it won't absorb water a second time. You may use wet foam for either thick or fragile stems, though it tends to clog the veins of certain fresh-cut flowers. Ask your florist for advice on specific blooms. Cut the block to fit the vase first;

leave enough space between the foam and the sides of the container so water can be added to the flowers. Float the foam in plenty of water for about 30 minutes, but don't force the saturation or air pockets will form in it. Wedge it into place. A wet-foam brick wicks water to the flowers, but be sure to add water lost by evaporation or consumed by the flowers. For any cut arrangement, add bottled water with preservative, since as little as 10 percent moisture loss causes flower wilting.

Now you're ready to begin. If you decide to construct a vase from raw materials, the easiest and fastest way to line or waterproof it is to place a smaller container inside it. A plastic milk jug, glass jar, or bud vase all work well. Or, if your container has an odd shape or size, simply hot glue or tape heavy plastic to the inside, then trim it. If, instead, you'd like to embellish a purchased vase, haunt flea markets, garden centers, and discount stores. As the projects in this book demonstrate, many of the craft techniques that are most familiar to you may be applied to existing ceramic and glass vases—especially the plain-Jane variety that florists like to use.

Artful Display

You needn't go to very great lengths to experience the joy that comes from the sight of one bloom or many in your home. Whether it's a symphony of containers or one clear note, the impromptu arrays shown here freshen the house and gladden the heart. It's quick, simple fun to create a vignette on a sill, or as a dinner-table focal point, or to brighten a long patio wall. And now that you know the secrets of success with vases and flowers, almost any container can be part of a blithe celebration of nature.

Unify various elements in a grouping by making sure they share at least one similarity, whether it's color, texture, or shape. Put miniature flowers in a grouping of cut-glass salt cellars. Fill an antique aluminum mold with bundled grasses. For a lone blossom, give your sense of whimsy free reign. Tuck an antique perfume bottle—or a dime-store toothbrush holder—into any nook where the light and the setting show it off. Or float a brilliant blossom in a low ceramic bowl. Let the cuttings lean, curve, and twist in their own inimitable way. Whatever means you use to create your artful display, think of the two together as poetic sculpture, if only for a little while.

Black Vinyl

Designer: Joan K. Morris

Spare and strong, this black vinyl and aluminum sleeve gives an ordinary florist's glass cylinder vase so much more muscle.

Materials & Tools

Cylindrical glass vase, 9 x 5 inches (22.9 x 12.7 cm)

1 x 3-inch (2.5 x 7.6 cm) piece of black vinyl flooring

Scissors

Aluminum foil tape, ½ inch (1.3 cm) wide

Hot-glue gun and glue sticks

66 washers, ¾ inch (2.9 cm) each

Instructions

1 Cut the vinyl into a rectangle measuring 9 x 16 inches (22.9 x 40.6 cm).

2 Wrap the vinyl around the vase. Where the end overlaps itself, cut the edge along the line of the circle.

3 Cut a piece of the foil 16 inches (40.6 cm) long. Fold the foil in half lengthwise, and fold it over the top edge of the vinyl.

4 With the vase standing, wrap the vinyl around it with the foil at the top. Glue down the overlap.

5 Lay the vase on its side. Working only on the face-up side, glue washers onto the circles' centers. Let the glue set on each row before turning the vase. Repeat until all the circles have washers glued to them.

Floral Frame

Designer: Terry Taylor

It's simple to create a modern, floral still life without being a master of botanical painting. Okay, you'll have to paint the frame—but not the blossom!

Materials & Tools

Flat-profile wooden picture frame

Paint

Paintbrush

Cyanoacrylate glue

Plastic hose clamp (available at home improvement stores)

Wood screw

Screwdriver

Test tube

Instructions

1 Paint the picture frame with the paint and the paintbrush. Let it dry.

2 Put a small amount of the cyanoacrylate glue on the back of the hose clamp. Attach the clamp to the bottom center of the frame.

3 Screw the wood screw into the frame to secure the clamp.

4 Place the test tube in the clamp. If it feels a bit loose, add a drop of glue to secure it to the clamp.

5 Hang the frame on the wall, fill the vase with water, and add the perfect blossom or small bouquet.

Terra-Cotta Relief

Designer: Joan K. Morris

Embossed metal and hot, deep color really
spice up an ordinary terra-cotta pot.

Materials & Tools

Terra-cotta pot, 7½ inches (19 cm) in diameter

Magenta paint

Paintbrush

Spray pot sealant, available at home improvement stores

Aluminum flashing

Tin snips

Contact adhesive (for ceramics and metal)

Ruler

Embossing tool, such as a skewer, ballpoint, or an orangewood cuticle stick

Dense foam or old mouse pad, ½ inch (1.3 cm) thick

Scrap piece of wood

Ball-peen hammer

Black paint

Clear semi-gloss polyurethane sealant

Instructions

1 Paint the area of the pot below the rim with the magenta paint. Let that coat dry and add another.

2 Spray the pot with the sealant, inside and out, following the manufacturer's instructions. Let it dry, and repeat the process several times.

3 Trace the outside circumference of the bottom of the pot onto a piece of paper. Use the tin snips to cut a circle from the aluminum flashing. Cut a second circle, slightly smaller than the outside dimension of the pot, for its interior.

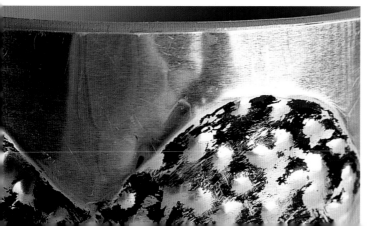

4 With the contact adhesive, glue the larger circle to the outside bottom of the pot. Fill in the hole on the bottom of the pot with adhesive.

5 Put a bead of adhesive around the hole in the bottom of the pot. Glue the second circle of flashing onto the bottom of the pot.

6 Cut a piece of the aluminum flashing 4 x 22 inches (10.2 x 55.9 cm).

7 Measure ½ inch (1.3 cm) in from the edges of the shorter ends of the flashing. Using the ruler and the embossing tool, draw a line ½ inch (1.3 cm) in from each end. Place the aluminum on the foam, and redraw the line several times, pressing hard. Fold over the ½-inch (1.3 cm) "hems," then use the edge of the tool to press down on the folds.

8 To create a template, draw a design on paper. With the "wrong" side up (i.e., the hem face-up), place the aluminum flashing on the foam. Put the paper template on top, and use the embossing tool to trace the edges of the design. Remove the paper, and, pressing hard, go over the design until you've achieved the desired effect.

9 Place the aluminum face-down on the scrap of wood. Pound the inside of the design with the ball-peen hammer to create the circles.

10 Paint the entire inside area of the design with the black paint, then wipe it off, leaving some of the black in the crevices. Let it dry.

11 Paint the semi-gloss polyurethane over the black-painted area. Let it dry, then repeat.

12 Place the aluminum flashing around the pot. Cut it so that the ends butt together. Adhere the flashing onto the pot.

Indigo Glass Mosaic

Designer: Jill MacKay

Express your mood indigo with richly colored bits of glass set, jewel-like, into a deeply pigmented grout.

Materials & Tools

Clear glass cylinder vase, 9 inches (22.9 cm) tall

Safety goggles and dust mask

Glass cutter, glass mosaic cutter, and tile nippers

Stained glass in a variety of blues, purples, and some clear pieces

Old towel

Waterproof silicone adhesive in a bottle with a with a nozzle tip

Razor blade

16 ounces (.45 kg) fortified white sanded latex grout

2 small plastic containers or buckets

Purple and blue pure pigments, or acrylic paint

Rubber or latex gloves

Paper clip

Plastic sheeting

Sponge

Soft cloth for polishing

Instructions

1 Wearing your safety goggles, use the glass cutter and breaking pliers to score and cut all the glass into strips, approximately ¼ to ½ inch (6 mm to 1.3 cm) wide, in lengths varying from 4 to 6 inches (10.2 to 15.2 cm).

2 Choose a strip of glass, and use the glass mosaic cutters to nip it into smaller pieces that range from ½ to 2 inches (1.3 to 5.1 cm). Keep the pieces of the strip in the order that you cut them.

3 Rest the vase on its side on an old towel. Deposit a line of glue down the length of each individual piece of glass. Put on enough so that it will cover the bottom when it's pressed down firmly but not enough to squeeze out the sides. (If this happens, clean off the excess with the end of a paper clip.)

4 Starting ½ inch (1.3 cm) from the bottom of the vase, firmly press an end piece from a nipped strip onto the vase, making sure it's in a vertical position. Glue on the strips, working your way up from the bottom each time. Leave ¹⁄₁₆ to ⅛ inch (1.6 to 3 mm) of space between pieces and between each of the strips. Vary the placement of the different colors and the height of each strip. Work your way around the vase, giving each section time to dry before turning the vase. Let the vase dry overnight.

5 Use the razor blade to carefully clean off any bits of dried glue. Wearing your dust mask, add just enough water to ¾ pound (.34 kg) of dry grout to form a mixture with the consistency of thick oatmeal. Use your gloved hands for mixing. Color the grout to your liking with pigment.

6 Working over the plastic sheeting, firmly press grout over the surface of the upright vase. Carefully use your fingertips to surround the upper and lower edges with at least ½-inch border (1.3 cm) of grout. Smooth and flatten these edges.

7 Wipe away the excess grout with a damp sponge, but be careful not to disturb the top or bottom edges. Let the grout dry for 10 to 15 minutes.

8 To define the upper edge, slowly pull the razor blade through the grout, cutting away just enough to create a smooth curving edge. Carefully remove the excess. If you see that the grout has pulled up from the surface of the vase, smooth it back down. Smooth the bottom edge with your fingertip.

9 Clean and polish the surface of the glass with the soft cloth; use the razor blade for stubborn spots. Smooth the top edge of the grout as much as possible without dislodging it.

10 Wrap the vase in plastic, and let set for three days to let the grout cure. When needed, wash the vase with a damp sponge; it isn't dishwasher safe.

Scandinavian Wood

Designer: Diana Light

Become a master pyrographer the first time you try it. The secret to this wood-block design is that it contains a science-lab glass vial to hold water.

Materials & Tools

4 square wooden blocks with 3-inch (7.6 cm) sides

220-grit sandpaper

Palm or hand sander (optional)

Electric wood-burning tool

Flow tip

Shading tip

Ruler

Drill

Wood-boring bit, 1 inch (2.5 cm) in diameter

Glass vial, 1 x 9¾ inches (2.5 x 24.7 cm), available from a science lab supplier

Craft glue

Instructions

1 With the sandpaper, remove any rough edges on the blocks.

2 Line up the four blocks. Draw a curving pencilled line from the bottom block to within 1¼ inches (3.2 cm) from the top one. Draw the same line on all four sides.

3 Trace over the lines with the flow tip on the wood-burning tool.

4 Use the shading point to add leaves onto the lines. Alternate the placement of the leaves along the stem; add a final leaf at the top of each line. Use the shading tip to add some dark areas to the leaves' interiors.

5 Use the ruler to mark the exact center of the top and bottom blocks. Drill through the top three blocks with the wood-boring bit.

6 Put the vial through the first three blocks. Drill through the center of the fourth block until you have a hole just deep enough for the bottom of the vial to fit into. The neck should be flush with the top of the top block.

7 Once the vial is fitted to the bottom block, remove the vial and coat the hole with craft glue. Replace the vial and let it dry.

23

Decalomania

Designer: Robin Schoenfeld

Get a fabulous look on brushed or shiny aluminum with
images copied onto ultra-thin decal transfer paper.

Materials & Tools

Aluminum vase in brushed or shiny finish (home decorating stores stock these in assorted sizes and shapes)

Assortment of images for transfer

Scissors

Image decal transfer paper

Small basin of warm water

Squeegee replacement blade, cut into 3-inch (7.6 cm) lengths

Paper towels

Blow dryer or heat gun

Home oven

Clear varnish for decorative metal painting projects (optional)

Instructions

1 Select the images you want to use, cut them out, and tape them to a piece of blank paper for copying. Arrange them closely together on the sheet, so that you can copy as many images at one time as possible.

2 Have the images transferred onto the decal paper by a commercial copy shop. It helps to select a smaller privately owned copy shop that is accustomed to doing T-shirt transfers or other specialized copying work. (Caution: Only low-heat copiers may be used with the paper, and ink-jet printers not at all. Follow the manufacturer's instructions carefully.)

3 Gather together the basin of water, scissors, squeegee blade, and paper towels. Cut a copied image from the sheet of images and set the remainder aside, well away from the water. Drop the first image into the basin. It immediately will curl into a scroll shape as the water soaks into the gummed backing paper and begins to detach itself from the transparent decal on top. Make sure the image is completely submerged. Soak the material 30 seconds to 1 minute, and remove it from the water.

4 Lay the decal on the paper towels, image side down. Gently slide away the backing paper, revealing about half of the decal beneath. (It should slide easily; if the backing paper catches and drags, return it to the water. Additional soaking will loosen the adhesive completely.)

5 Lay the image against the vase, image side up. Anchor the decal at one edge, holding it against the vase with one hand while gently pulling the backing paper out from under it with the other hand. Smooth the image down to the surface with your fingers. Use the squeegee blade to gently press water and air bubbles from under the image. Soak up excess moisture with the paper towels. The decal may crease around the edges of a larger image being applied to a concave surface; these can be smoothed out. Use hot water from the tap in your basin to soak the images; then gently stretch the softened decal to fit the curves. You also can use a blow dryer or heat gun to remove creases from the images once they have been squeegeed to the surface. Heat any creased areas, and tap them flat with your fingertips. (Be careful to keep electrical appliances well away from the water basin.) Repeat the process with the rest of the images, layering them over one another to cover the surface of the vase. Turn some images sideways or upside down for an interesting effect.

6 Remove any racks from your oven before standing the vase upright in it. Heat it to 350°F for 10 to 15 minutes, or until the images look shiny instead of matte. Turn off the oven and let the vase cool while it's still inside. (Caution: Using potholders will leave fabric impressions in the hot, melted film of the decals.) Once they're cooled, however, they're very durable.

7 If you'd like additional protection for the design, paint your vase with a thin coat of a clear varnish intended for use with decorative metal-painting projects, available at craft stores.

Copper Bands

Designer: Terry Taylor

Turquoise and copper—two raw
materials mined in the Southwest—are
a vibrant color combination. This vase
is an urban interpretation of a
Southwestern theme.

Materials & Tools

Glass vase

Copper mesh

Scissors

Hot-glue gun and glue sticks

Turquoise beads

Copper wire

Instructions

1 Wrap the copper mesh around the vase. Cut it to the height you wish with the scissors, then cut the mesh to the length you need plus a small amount of overlap. Set it aside.

2 Measure and cut 1-inch (2.5-cm) strips long enough to wrap around the vase.

3 Wrap the mesh around the vase. Hot glue it in place at the overlap.

4 Wrap the copper strips around the vase. Hot glue them to the mesh.

5 Thread the beads onto lengths of copper wire.

6 Hot glue the beads to the copper strips. Bring the wire to the back of the vase, and twist the ends together. Trim the ends of the wire with scissors.

Designer: Terry Taylor

Hardware Chic Cross-Stitch

To get this sassy look, the designer added funky embellishments to a plastic container in a hot color.

Materials & Tools

Square plastic vase

Rubber washers of different sizes

Pencil and paper (optional)

Scissors

Cyanoacrylate glue

Instructions

1 Play with different arrangements of the washers on the vase. Arrange them randomly or in a pattern. When you have decided on the design, sketch it out or set the arrangement on a flat surface.

2 Cut each washer in half with the scissors. (You can use the washers whole if desired.)

3 Glue the washers to the vase with cyanoacrylate glue. Let the glue dry.

Meshed Stencil

Designer: Terry Taylor

The tiny squares in this spray-on design cleverly echo the shape of this used-to-be-plain vase. Now it really says something!

Materials & Tools

Straight-sided vase

Drywall mesh tape, available at hardware stores

Scissors

Waxed paper

Spray paint

Instructions

1 Cut the drywall mesh tape into strips with the scissors. Adhere a strip of tape to the vase. Use a small sheet of waxed paper on top of the strip to press down hard on the mesh tape with your fingers. Repeat the process with the remaining strips.

2 Spray a light coat of paint on the vase. Don't try to cover the vase with a solid, heavy coat. Let the paint dry.

3 If desired, spray a second coat on the vase. You may need to re-press the tape to the vase.

29

Odes on Urns
(With Apologies to Mr. Keats)

Designer: Terry Taylor

Anyone can have a Grecian urn (Portland vase or classic Roman style) in their home with these imaginative cover-ups. "O Attic shape! Fair attitude!"

Materials & Tools

Glass cylinder vase

Black-and-white clip-art images

Black foam-core board

Spray adhesive

Craft knife

Hot-glue gun and glue sticks

Instructions

1 Select your clip-art image. You can find many copyright-free images on the Internet or in books devoted to clip art. Examine older books in the public library for vintage images to photocopy as well.

2 Photocopy and enlarge the image as desired. You'll need two images for each vase cover-up. Adhere the photocopies to the foam-core board with the spray adhesive. Use the craft knife to cut out the images.

3 Cut two 2-inch-wide (5 cm) spacer strips from foam-core board. They must be a little longer than the diameter measurement of the vase, so the vase will be able to fit between the two sides of the cover-up.

4 Hot glue the strips between the two images, and slip the vase between the strips.

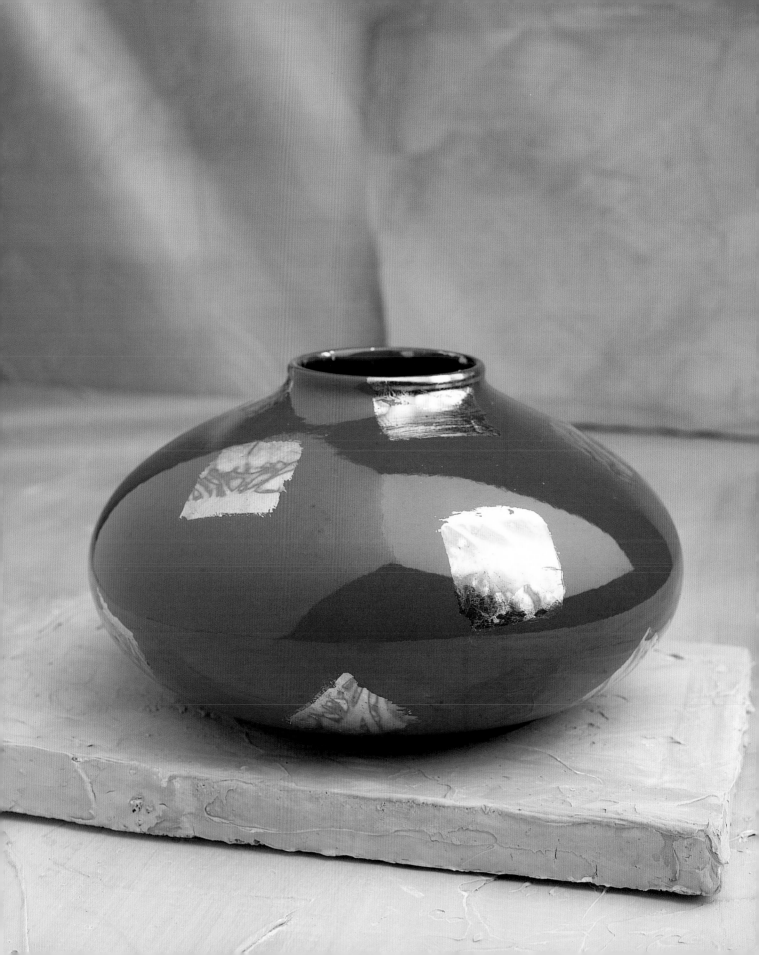

Gold-Leaf Patchwork

Designer: Terry Taylor

Variegated composition leaf is the perfect counterpoint to the rich oxblood red of this vase. The simplicity of the decoration works well with the elegant Oriental lines of the vase.

Materials & Tools

Low, flared-body glass vase

Variegated composition gold leaf

Scissors

Metal-leaf adhesive

Small paintbrush

Soft cosmetic brush

Instructions

1 Cut out squares of the composition leaf. It's easier to cut the leaf if you keep it sandwiched between the tissue sheets in the book.

2 Brush the adhesive onto the vase with the small paintbrush in shapes approximately the same size as the squares of leaf. Let the adhesive dry.

3 Carefully lift a square of leaf and slide it onto the vase.

4 Use the soft cosmetic brush to stipple the leaf onto the adhesive. Brush away any leaf that doesn't adhere.

I-Ching

Designer: Allison Smith

Using Chinese coins and ceramic beads, designer Allison Smith wrapped this vase with Oriental flair.

Materials & Tools

Tall, cinched-waist vase

2 yards (1.8 m) of thin olive green leather cord

Scissors

1 large Chinese coin

3 small Chinese coins

3 small square ceramic Chinese beads

Instructions

1 Divide the leather cord into thirds, and cut it with the scissors.

2 Gather the cords together in a bunch. Thread one end through the center of the large Chinese coin. Wrap the other end around the vase, then through the hole in the center of the coin. Keep the ends of the cords even and the coin flush against the front of the vase. Gather the ends and tie them into a knot.

3 Alternately thread the small coins and the ceramic beads onto the ends of the leather cords. Vary the length at which they hang.

4 Tie the ends with simple knots and trim the excess cord.

Jute Lace

Designer: Terry Taylor

This basic cover-up conceals a water-proof container. After learning this simple construction technique, you can embellish it any way you like.

Materials & Tools

Vase or watertight container

Metal-edge ruler

140 lb. watercolor paper or poster board

Bone folder

Craft knife

Hole punch

Eyelets and eyelet punch

Jute

Cellophane tape (optional)

Instructions

1 Determine what you want the final size of the container's base and sides to be. (For your first container, a square base design is easier. This vase has a 2-inch-square (5 cm) base with sides that angle out to 4 inches (10.2 cm) wide at the top; the sides are 3 inches (7.6 cm) tall.

2 Now you'll draw a grid on the stiff paper. First, use the metal edge to draw a line, parallel to the paper's edge, that is 3 inches (7.6 cm) in from the edge. Draw a second parallel line 2 inches (5 cm) from the first one. Finally, draw a third parallel line 3 inches (7.6 cm) from the second one. Turn the paper 90 degrees and repeat the process.

3 Alter the grid to make sides that are slightly wider at the top than at the base. At the grid's outer edges, make marks 1 inch (2.5 cm) out from the lines that are 2 inches (5 cm) apart. Use the metal-edge ruler to connect the marks from the outer edges in to the corners of the base, as shown below.

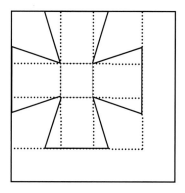

4 Use the tip of the bone folder to score the lines of the square base. Cut out the pattern.

5 Mark a line of dots (use an odd number) on a piece of paper for the holes you'll punch along each side. Use this template to mark each side, to ensure that all the holes will be aligned with each other. Punch the marked holes with the hole punch.

6 Use the hand-held eyelet punch to set the eyelets along each side.

7 Cut four lengths of jute, each measuring four times the height of the sides. (To lace a tall shape, wind a bit of tape on each end of your jute to prevent it from raveling.) Start lacing at the top of two adjacent sides. Bring the ends through the eyelets from the inside, then cross the laces to opposite sides, just as you would when you lace your shoes. Gradually pull the adjacent sides together as you work your way to the base. End the lacing on the inside of the container, knot the jute, and trim it closely. Lace all the sides this way. Use a small watertight vase inside the cover-up.

Happy Vinyl Bouquet

Designer: Joan K. Morris

Bring this playful "vase"
design along when you visit
a friend, and leave it behind
as a gift.

Materials & Tools

Plastic or vinyl place mat

Ruler

2 yards (1.8 m) pink electrical wire

Wire cutter

2 yards (1.8 m) clear plastic tubing, ¼ inch (6 mm) wide

Utility knife

Cyanoacrylate glue

Clear glass vase, ½ x 7 inches (1.3 x 17.8 cm)

Hole punch

Instructions

1 Measure a long side of the place mat, and cut the electrical wire with the wire cutters to that length.

2 Use the utility knife to cut the clear tubing to the same length as the wire, plus 2 inches (5 cm). Slit the tube down its entire length. Be careful not to cut it in half.

3 Roll the place mat into a cone shape with the right side out. There are many possible shapes, so play with it until you find one you like. Adhere the edges with the glue. Follow the glue manufacturer's instructions for the setting time.

4 With the scissors, round off the top front point of the place mat.

5 Glue the pink wire onto the upper front edge of the place mat.

6 Place the cut tube over both the wire and the top edge of the place mat. Overlap the ends in the back.

7 Glue the inside of the tube and place mat. Shape the top of the place mat. If you like, you can flatten the back edge somewhat so that it's not so rounded.

8 Cut a piece of wire 24 inches (61 cm) long and cut a piece of tubing 21 inches (53.3 cm) long. Slide the wire into the tube, letting 1½ inches (3.8 cm) of it extend from each end of the tubing.

9 Use the hole punch to make two holes on each side of the place mat. Place the first one ½ inch (1.3 cm) from the top edge and the second one ½ inch (1.3 cm) below the first.

10 Starting from the inside, lace the wire that extends from one end of the tubing through the top hole to the outside, then back inside through the lower hole, on both sides of the place mat.

11 Adhere the wire to the inside edge of the vase. Shape the wire to the inside of the vase. Adjust the shape of the wire handle so that it will hang properly. Place the smaller vase inside it.

Oriental Wrap

Designer: Terry Taylor

The contrasts in shape, materials, and textures of this wrapper totally transform an otherwise ordinary glass container.

Materials & Tools

Glass cylinder vase

Paper

Corrugated paper

Craft knife

Asian newspaper or printed paper

Handmade paper

Scissors

Glue

Cord (leather, silk, linen, or hemp)

Hot-glue gun and glue sticks

Chinese coin

Instructions

1 Wrap a sheet of paper around your vase to determine the circumference. Add at least ½ inch (1.3 cm) to the measurement just to be safe.

2 Cut the corrugated paper with the craft knife to match the circumference you measured. Cut the paper to the desired height.

3 Lay the corrugated paper flat. Cut out smaller pieces of both the printed and the handmade papers with the scissors. Glue them to the corrugated paper. Let the glue dry.

4 Wrap the corrugated paper around the vase. Hot glue the paper to the vase.

5 Wrap lengths of the cord around the vase from the back to the front. Thread the coin onto the cords and tie them in a decorative knot.

6 Hot glue the coin to the front of the vase.

Bamboo Wrap

Designer: Allison Smith

The designer found inspiration for this vase cover-up in the kitchen-notions department. All the elements are coordinated to her Eastern theme.

Materials & Tools

Cylinder glass vase

Metal can

Rust-colored spray paint

Flexible tape measurer

Scissors

Bamboo place mat

Brown leather cord, 1 yard (.9 m)

2 disk-shaped bone beads

2 round bone beads

Instructions

1 Paint the can with the rust-colored spray paint.

2 Measure the height and circumference of the can with the flexible tape measurer. Using the scissors, cut the bamboo place mat to the height of the can.

3 Trim the binding off one edge of the place mat. Remove several of the bamboo slats, then tie the extra string along the edge to secure the mat and keep the bamboo from unraveling. Add 1 inch to the circumference measurement you took in step 2, and cut the width of the mat to this measurement.

4 Remove ³/₄ inch (1.9 cm) of the bamboo strips from the cut end. Roll the mat around the can to make sure it fits. You may need to add or subtract a bamboo strip in order to make sure it covers the can completely. Tie the excess string in order to keep the mat from unraveling.

5 Wrap the mat around the can, and tie the ends of the strings together on the back of the can. Trim the excess string. Tightly wrap the leather cord twice around the bamboo mat. Keep the ends even and tie them into a nice large bow. Thread the bone beads onto the ends of the leather cord and secure them with a knot. Trim the ends.

Designer: Terry Taylor

Foolproof Tissue Découpage

What's not to love about this vase? Can you cut and glue? There you go—an absolutely fabulous, foolproof way to perk up any flower container.

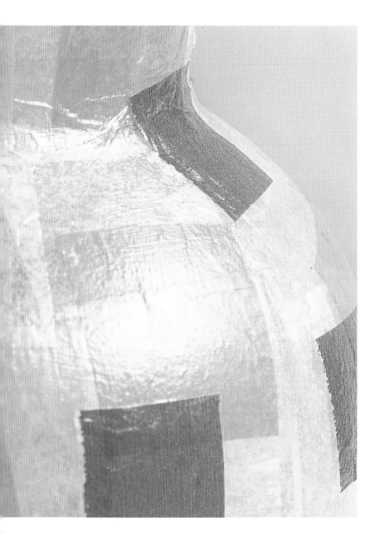

Materials & Tools

Tissue papers

Scissors

Découpage medium

Vase

Paintbrush

Instructions

1 Use the scissors to cut right through the folded lengths of the tissue paper (straight from the package), making tissue strips. Cut the folded strips into square shapes. Separate the colors into like piles.

2 Paint the découpage medium onto a small area of the vase with the paintbrush. Glue a single color of shapes onto the body of the vase, overlapping them slightly. Allow the tissue to dry. If desired, make a second layer of the background color.

3 Brush the découpage medium onto the vase and randomly place other colors of tissue squares over the background layer.

4 Give the vase a final coat of découpage medium.

5 Let it dry completely. Foolproof and fabulous.

Curlicue Repoussé

Designer: Debba Haupert

Metal foil répoussé takes whimsical flights of fancy in this sweet square construction by designer Debba Haupert.

Materials & Tools

Mint green embossing foil

Medium-size square plastic box

Scissors

Sheet foam or magazine

Tape

Leaf stencils

Stylus

Silver metallic wax

Soft cloth for buffing

Double-sided adhesive sheets

Silver cord

Drill and a ⅛-inch (3-mm) bit

Heavy-duty wire cutters

Armature wire, ⅛ inch (3 mm) diameter, available in craft stores

Pliers

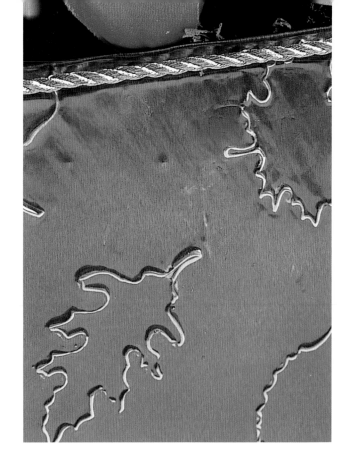

Instructions

1 Cut the embossing foil with the scissors to a long rectangle shape equal to the box's circumference, plus ¼ inch (6 mm), and equal to the box's height, plus ½ inch (1.3 cm). Place the foil, silver side up, on the foam or a magazine. Tape the leaf stencils in a random pattern onto the foil and trace around them with the stylus. With the soft cloth, apply the wax to the green side of the foil. Rub it with the cloth to remove the color from the embossed areas; then lightly buff it.

2 Line the silver side of the foil with pieces of adhesive sheet cut to fit, then adhere them to the plastic box, folding the ¼ inch (6-mm) excess over the top and bottom. Firmly press the foil with the cloth to fully adhere it to the container. Embellish the top of the container by tying a silver cord around it.

3 Drill a hole, ⅛ inch (3 mm) from each corner, in the bottom.

4 For the box's legs, cut two 16-inch (40.6-cm) pieces of armature wire. Gently bend one piece of wire in half to find the center point, then insert each end through the holes in two opposite corners of the bottom, so that equal amounts of the wire extend from the base of the container. With the pliers, twist the wire to form a tight spiral, then loop it back to the box. Repeat with the other end of the wire. Make the other two legs the same way. Adjust the wire, if necessary, so that the box sits level on a flat surface.

Teacups & Saucers

Designer: Joan K. Morris

This ingenious, stacked china cup-and-saucer tower has a five-hole frog built right into it. A perfect display for your next tea party.

Materials & Tools

2 saucers

2 teacups

Fine-point permanent marker

Safety glasses

Drill with ceramic or ½-inch (1.3-cm) bit

Waterproof contact adhesive (for ceramics)

Instructions

1 Mark the centers of the saucers with the marker. Staying ¼ inch (6 mm) from the edge of the depression, make four more marks in a circle around the center mark.

2 Wearing safety glasses, drill ½-inch-wide (1.3-cm) holes at each mark on the saucer. Take your time. (If you've never drilled ceramics before, you might want to first practice on a broken piece of china.) Repeat the process for the other saucer.

3 Turn one of the cups upside down, and place a drilled saucer on top of it. Mark matching holes onto the cup. Drill holes in the cup.

4 Place a drilled cup on the drilled saucer, and line up the holes. Use contact adhesive to adhere them together, with their holes aligned. Follow the manufacturer's instructions for the adhesive. Let it dry. Adhere the other cup and saucer together.

5 Glue the drilled cup-and-saucer unit to the other one. Let the piece dry for 24 hours before adding any water to it.

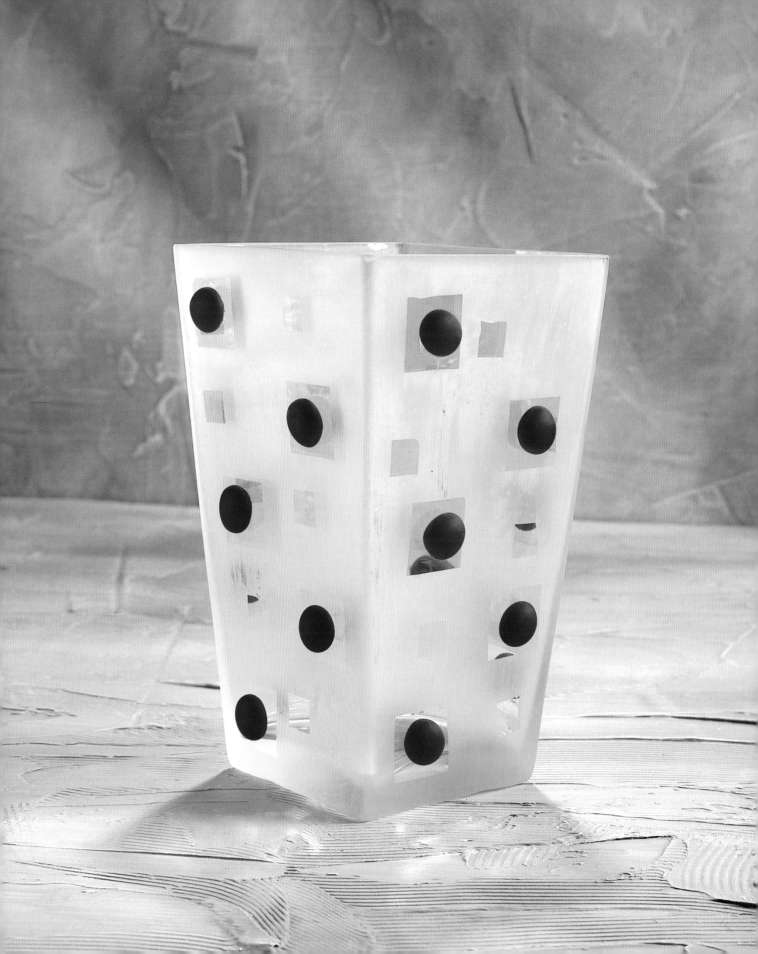

Cobalt Jewels

Designer: Terry Taylor

This etched-glass vase softens light that passes through it, while the gems provide an understated, glowing motif.

Materials & Tools

Square glass vase, 14 inches (35.6 cm) tall

Scissors

Self-adhesive shelf liner

Plastic spoon or knife

Etching cream

Glass jewels

Adhesive suitable for use with glass

Instructions

1 Clean all the surfaces of the glass vase. Use the scissors to cut large squares from the adhesive liner, measuring 1 inch (2.5 cm) on each side. Set them aside. Cut out smaller squares from the adhesive liner.

2 Remove the backing from a square of adhesive liner and adhere it to the vase. Use a plastic spoon or knife to firmly press down the edges of the adhesive liner. Adhere additional large and small squares to one side of the vase.

3 Follow the manufacturer's instructions to apply the etching cream to one side of the vase. Use the plastic spoon or knife to spread the etching cream. When the cream has been on the exposed area for the recommended amount of time, rinse it according to the manufacturer's instructions.

4 Repeat steps 2 and 3 on the remaining sides of the vase, one side at a time.

5 Lay the vase on its side. Glue a glass jewel in each large un-etched shape. Let the adhesive dry, following the manufacturer's instructions. Rotate the vase, and glue the jewels to the next side, allowing it to dry before moving to the next side. Make sure the adhesive is completely cured before using the vase.

Elegant Copper Wrap

Designer: Debba Haupert

Use a tall, narrow vase inside this sleeve-style constructed vase, ingeniously made from inexpensive home-improvement materials.

Materials & Tools

8-inch (20.3 cm) glass cylinder vase

Aluminum flashing, 10 x 12 inches (25.4 x 30.5 cm), available at home improvement stores

Heavy scissors

Protective gloves

18 inches (45.7 cm) of copper tubing, ¼ inch (6-mm) outside diameter, available at home improvement stores

Tube cutter

Instructions

Designer's Note

For more embellishment, try adding thin copper wire with beads. You can use the same materials and techniques to create matching napkin rings.

1 Cut the flashing with the scissors. Wear protective gloves to protect yourself from the sharp corners and edges.

2 Cut the tubing with the tube cutter.

3 Gently curve the tubing into a spiral with a 4- to 6-inch (10.2–15.2-cm) diameter.

4 Roll up the flashing along the 12-inch (30.5-cm) side, then insert it into the curved tubing. When released, the flashing will expand to fit inside the tubing.

Beaded Curtains

Designer: Diana Light

Diana Light took her inspiration from the basic materials of the unadorned vase to create these lovely metal and glass bead "curtains."

Materials & Tools

Pair of frosted-glass vases in metal stands, each 8 inches (20.3 cm) tall

Glass beads

Metal spacer beads

25 feet (7.6 m) of 7-strand flexible beading wire, .018 inch (0.46 mm) in diameter

Wire cutters

84 crimp beads

Needle-nose pliers or crimping pliers

Instructions

1 Each of the three sections of the stand holds seven bead strands. Arrange the beads in seven strands whose length is proportionate to the height of the vase. Refer to the photo, or devise your own bead pattern. The middle strand is the longest and the only one without a match. The other six strands are matching pairs, each pair becoming progressively shorter.

2 Cut a length of beading wire at least 2½ inches (6 cm) longer than the length of the middle strand. Slide a crimp bead almost to the end of the wire. Fold the end over, and push it back through the crimp bead. Squash the crimp with the needle-nose pliers.

3 String the beads onto the beading wire, starting at the bottom. At the end of each strand add another crimp bead. Wrap the wire around the vase's metal stand, then put it back through the crimp bead. Pull the wire tight and close the crimp bead. Hide the end of the wire in the strand of beads.

4 Repeat steps 1 through 3 for each section of the vase.

Abalone Wrap

Designer: Allison Smith

Pretty abalone buttons give this trio of etched bud vases an understated focal point.

Materials & Tools

3 tall bud vases

Measuring tape

Painter's tape, 1 inch (2.5 cm) wide

Cutting mat

Straight edge

Craft knife

Sponge craft brush

Etching cream

Waxed linen string in three different colors

3 abalone buttons, 1½ inches (3.8 cm) each

Instructions

1 Measure down 2 inches (5 cm) from the top of the first vase. Wrap a piece of painter's tape around the vase to mark the spot.

2 Tear off ten 10-inch (25.4-cm) pieces of the tape and place them on the cutting mat. Use the straight edge and the craft knife to cut the pieces in half lengthwise.

3 One at a time, place the strips of tape onto the vase vertically from the top horizontal tape to the base of the vase. Leave approximately ½ inch (1.3 cm) of exposed glass between each piece of tape. Firmly rub the tape to attach it to the glass.

4 With the sponge craft brush, paint the etching cream onto all exposed glass below the horizontal piece of tape. Allow the cream to process according to the manufacturer's directions, then rinse it off with cool water. Don't let the cream come into contact with your skin.

5 Remove the tape, then wash the vase with warm water.

6 Thread one end of the waxed linen string through the first abalone button, leaving about 3 inches (7.6 cm) of the string at the end for tying.

7 Wrap the linen around the vase above the etching, then thread it back through the buttonholes.

8 Pull the string taut and wrap it around the vase two more times.

9 Tie the string tightly behind the button. Cut and tuck in the ends of the string.

10 Repeat steps 1 through 9 on the remaining vases. Tie each with a different color of waxed linen.

Beaded Belt

Designer: Diana Light

Some of the earth's most beautiful materials—metal, wood, and semiprecious stones—are wrapped around this smart, cinched-waist ceramic vase.

Materials & Tools

Cinched-waist ceramic vase

Thin hemp twine

Scissors

Craft glue

Wooden beads

Coin with a hole in it

Wooden animal beads

Semiprecious stone beads

Instructions

Designer's Note

Take the hemp string with you when shopping to make sure the holes in the beads are big enough.

1 With the scissors, cut a length of twine 81 inches (2 m) long. Glue one end of it to the vase. Let it dry, then wrap the rest of it around the vase, using a little glue to secure it. Glue the other end to the vase.

2 Cut a piece of hemp about 24 inches (60 cm) long. Knot and string three small wooden beads at its center; tie a knot between each bead. Measure 1½ inches (3.8 cm), and repeat the pattern on both sides of the center. Wrap the beaded cord around the vase, and tie a square knot in the front.

3 Pull the hemp string ends through the coin, and use some glue to anchor it to the hemp. Let the glue dry.

4 Repeat the order of the small wooden beads and knots down both hemp strings. Add the wooden animal beads and the semiprecious stone beads at each end. Knot the ends of the strings and trim off any excess.

Flowering Gems

Designer: Jill MacKay

This clever technique uses clear glass gems to magnify tiny, gem-like flower images that were cut from garden magazines.

Materials & Tools

Flared-body clear glass vase, 7½ inches (19 cm) tall

Images of flowers, no larger than the diameter of the glass gems

Scissors

Clear glass gems in assorted sizes

Fine-tip permanent marker

Inexpensive craft paintbrush

Waterproof all-purpose, non-PVA glue

Cushion or towel

Clear silicone glue

Paper plate

Single-edge razor blade (optional)

Instructions

1 Select 30 glass gems. Look for the ones that have the smoothest bottoms and the clearest tops. Place a gem on top of the flower image you want to use, and trace around the gem with the permanent marker. Cut just inside the lines. Do this for all the gems.

2 With the paintbrush, paint a thin, even layer of waterproof glue on the bottom of a glass gem. Firmly press it onto a flower image, then pick up the gem and turn it over. Squeeze the excess glue from between the image and the gem with your fingertips until you can clearly see the entire image from the right side of the gem, and it no longer appears milky from the glue. Set it aside, glued side up, to dry. Repeat for all the gems.

3 Paint a layer of glue on the backside of all the images to strengthen them. Let them dry for several hours.

4 Practice adhering leftover clear gems with silicone glue onto the paper plate to find out how big a dab of glue you'll need. Put on enough so that it will cover the entire bottom when it's pressed down firmly but not enough to squeeze out from the sides. After it dries, trim away small bits of excess glue with the razor blade.

5 Lay the vase on its side, resting it on the towel or cushion so it won't roll. Use flower gems of similar size for the ring at the base of the neck. Work only on the face-up side of the vase, attaching several gems at the flattest place where the neck meets the body. While these are drying, glue lines of gems in graduated sizes onto the body. Let them dry for 10 to 15 minutes, or until you can turn the vase without detecting any slow slippage. Let each section dry thoroughly before you turn the vase or stand it up straight.

Red & White Hibiscus

Designer: Diana Light

The bold floral motif makes a strong graphic
statement. The design is very simple to apply
to a vase that has broad flat sides.

Materials & Tools

Triangular ceramic vase, 12 inches (30.5 cm) tall

Surface conditioner (if necessary)

Flat brush

Masking tape

Red opaque ceramic paint

White opaque ceramic paint

Template, photocopied at 100%

Ballpoint pen

Transfer paper

Small round brush

Towels (to rest vase in while painting
so it
doesn't roll over)

Instructions

 Clean and dry the vase. If the vase you're using requires it, cover the vase with the surface conditioner, using the flat brush. Let it dry.

2 Apply masking tape to the inside of the rim for a clean painted edge.

3 Follow the paint manufacturer's instructions for shaking or stirring the paints, then cover the outside of the vase with red paint, with all the brushstrokes in the same direction. Be sure to paint all the way to the masking tape on the inside of the rim. Let it dry. If needed, apply a second coat of paint, brushing it on in the opposite direction of the first layer, and let it dry.

4 Center and tape the transfer paper to the vase. Then tape the design you want to use on top. With the ballpoint pen, trace the design.

5 Remove the papers, and use the small round brush to fill in the design with white paint. Let it dry; apply a second coat.

6 Follow the manufacturer's instructions to cure the paint.

63

Slate & River Rock

Cool stone materials are perfectly balanced in this ikebana-style vase.

Materials & Tools

3 pieces of slate, 4 x 11 inches (10.2 x 27.9 cm), with 120-degree mitred corners

1 triangular piece of slate, 6½ x 6½ x 6½ inches (16.5 x 16.5 x 16.5 cm), with 120-degree mitred corners

Contact adhesive (for ceramics)

3 thick rubber bands

3 small river rocks of the same thickness

Level

Gray caulk

Instructions

Designer's Note

You should be able to have the slate cut and mitered where you buy it.

1 Apply contact adhesive, following the manufacturer's instructions, to each mitred edge of the three pieces. Stack the three pieces together and secure them with the rubber bands. Let them dry for 24 hours.

2 Center the three-sided construction on top of the triangle. Glue it into place and let it dry 24 hours.

3 Place the three river rocks under the corners of triangle. Set the level on top of the construction to make sure the vase stands straight and true. Glue the rocks into place and let them dry for 24 hours.

4 If needed, fill in some of the edges with gray caulk.

5 Use a liner inside vase if you want to use fresh flowers.

Embossed Copper

Designer: Livia McRee

Metal is so *chic*, and this design easily graces a sideboard or a patio table. Designer Livia McRee even includes a hanging loop.

Materials & Tools

Tin vase (available at craft stores and garden centers)

20-gauge copper wire

Fine-weave copper wire mesh (available at art and craft supply stores)

Embossing copper

Ball-ended stylus or wooden embossing tool (sold separately or with an embossing kit)

Permanent adhesive suitable for metal

Scalloped decorative paper cutter (optional)

Wire cutter or old, dull scissors

Instructions

1 Cut a length of wire 1½ times the circumference of the vase. Fold the wire in half. Twist the wire together twice, 2 inches (5 cm) below the fold, to form a loop.

2 Align the loop with the back of the vase, and wrap the ends of the wire around to the front. Twist the ends to secure them, making sure the twist is directly opposite of the loop, and snip off the excess wire. Press the ends flush with the vase.

3 Cut a square of wire mesh and a square of embossing copper. The embossing copper should be slightly smaller than the wire mesh. If you would like a decorative border, cut them with a special cutter.

4 Tape the embossing copper to a soft work surface, like an old magazine or a piece of non-corrugated cardboard. Sketch an embossing design on a paper square, and tape it over the copper. To create the slightly textured background here, the designer ran the stylus (always in the same direction) over the flat background areas on the front of the copper before embossing the image itself. Trace the image outlines with the stylus. Turn the copper over, and use the stylus to "fill in" the outlines, which will create the raised effect on the front side. Play with different ways of embossing the same image to see which works best.

5 Attach the embossed metal to the center of the mesh with permanent adhesive. Adhere the mesh to the center of the vase. Make sure it's centered along the wire wrap.

Curvaceous Lace

Designer: Jean Tomaso Moore

Outrageous, yes, but nonetheless perfect for the boudoir.

Materials & Tools

Curvy glass vase, 18 inches (45.7 cm) tall

1 pair of black lace pantyhose (preferably seamless) or knee-high stockings

Scissors

Strong, clear-drying glue

Small piece of lace trim to fit around the top rim of the vase

Instructions

1 Pull one leg of the lace pantyhose up to the top of the vase. Smooth the lace against the glass, stretching it as much as possible. Cut off the excess lace at the top of vase.

2 Apply a bead of glue around the rim of the vase and press the top of the stocking onto the glue. Trim away any excess material. Let the glue dry.

3 Neatly cover the top rim of the vase by gluing the smaller piece of lace around it. Press and smooth the lace in place with your fingertips.

Blue Willow China

Designer: Terry Taylor

Designer Terry Taylor used the ever-popular Blue Willow china pattern to create this charming, cottage-style vase from a low, open-neck bowl.

Materials & Tools

Ceramic bowl

Safety goggles or glasses

Variety of ceramic plates and saucers

Tile nippers

Polystyrene foam meat trays

Tile cement

White sanded grout

Mixing container for grout

Grout spreader and polyethylene foam wrap sheet (white packing material)

Instructions

Use white, solid blue, and Blue Willow pattern china. You'll need more than you think, so buy 10 or 15 plates at thrift stores and yard sales.

1 Prepare a supply of mosaic shards. Put on the safety goggles and use the tile nippers to break all the plates in half, unless they have a central medallion you'd like to use in your design. Remove the rims and trim them into small rectangular pieces. Break the flat portions of the plate into small pieces. Sort the pieces, using a different foam tray for each color.

2 Trim a plate with a Blue Willow medallion motif into a circular tile. Carefully use the tile nippers to remove small portions of the plate rim, working toward the raised foot of the plate. Trim the rims as you did in step 1, and set them aside. Use the tip of the tile nippers to trim away small parts of the raised foot until you have a round medallion tile.

3 Use the tile cement to adhere the medallion to the bowl. Then adhere the remaining tiles (but not the pieces from the rims) to the bowl, placing them close together.

4 Use the finished edges of the plate rims you trimmed in step 1 to create a finished edge on the rim of the bowl.

5 Allow the mosaic to dry overnight.

6 Mix the white sanded grout according to the manufacturer's instructions.

7 Use the grout spreader or the polyethylene foam wrap to spread the grout over the surface of the mosaic. Use enough pressure to force the grout into all of the spaces between the shards. Let the grout set up for about 15 minutes. Then, carefully remove the excess grout with the polyethylene foam wrap or clean lint-free rags. Follow the grout manufacturer's recommendations for removing the grout haze that develops.

8 Let the grout dry completely before using the vase.

Blue Leaves

Designer: Terry Taylor

Create subtle texture in a tone-on-tone treatment with skeletonized leaves.

Materials & Tools

Flat-sided vase

Waxed paper

Skeletonized leaves

Paintbrush

Découpage medium

Instructions

1 Tear off a sheet of the waxed paper. Lay it on a flat surface. Place one of the skeletonized leaves on the waxed paper. Use the paintbrush to coat it with the découpage medium.

2 Place the leaves on the vase.

3 Remove excess medium from around the edges if needed. Let the leaves dry.

4 Coat each leaf with a second coat of découpage medium to seal it to the vase.

5 Let the découpage medium dry completely before using the vase.

Suspension Wires

Designer: Lynn B. Krucke

Display a single bloom in all its glory when you hang this bottle vase in a sunny window.

Materials & Tools

Small glass bottle

Self-adhesive shelf liner

Leaf-shaped paper punch

Scissors

Glass etching cream

Paintbrush with acrylic bristles

22-gauge copper wire, 1 yard (3 m)

22-gauge green wire, 1 yard (3 m)

Clamp or table vise

Wire cutters

Round-nose pliers

Instructions

1 Thoroughly clean the bottle; oils and dirt interfere with the etching process.

2 Punch leaf shapes from the shelf liner with the paper punch. Cut around the punched shapes with the scissors, creating small stencils.

3 Remove the backing paper, and apply the stencils to the clean bottle. Use the cloth to press the stencils in place to keep dirt and oil off the glass.

4 Follow the manufacturer's safety precautions and instructions for using the cream. Use the paintbrush to apply a thick layer of etching cream to the area of the glass within each stencil, and let it set. Remove the etching cream and the stencils. Rinse and dry the bottle.

5 Hold the two lengths of wire together as one, and fold them in half. Clamp all four loose ends of wire together in the vise or table clamp.

6 Insert a pencil in the loops at the other end of the wires. Turn the pencil to twist them all together. Remove the wire from the vise, and trim off the loop with the wire cutters.

7 Securely twist a hanging loop at the center of the twisted wire. Hold the hanging loop at one side of the bottle, and wrap the wire ends around the bottle's neck several times, twisting them together each time they cross.

8 Use the round-nose pliers to shape the wire ends into spirals, then press them against the bottle.

Three Precious Metals

Designer: Allison Smith

Take color and texture contrasts to new heights when you make over cobalt-blue bud vases with metallic foil.

Materials & Tools

3 blue glass vases

Foil leaf adhesive

Small round paintbrush

Copper, gold, and silver foil leaf

Foil leaf sealer

Instructions

1 Paint a thin line of foil leaf adhesive around the first vase 1 inch (2.5 cm) down from the top and another line 1 inch (2.5 cm) from the bottom.

2 Dip the wooden end of the paintbrush into the adhesive and dot it onto the vase, making small polka dots.

3 Allow the adhesive to dry until it's clear. Wash the adhesive from the paintbrush.

4 Carefully place a sheet of foil leaf onto the vase. Gently rub it with your hands until it's burnished into the adhesive. The foil leaf won't stick to the areas that are free of adhesive.

5 Rinse the vase under cool water. Allow it to dry.

6 Repeat steps 1 through 5 on the remaining vases, using a different color of leaf for each one.

7 Seal the leaf on each vase with the foil leaf sealer.

Ikebana-Style Stacked Stone

A perfect fit with nature,
in classic ikebana fashion.

Materials & Tools

Metal floral frog

Ceramic, glass or plastic cup large enough to house the frog and a small amount of water

2-part epoxy adhesive

Several large pond stones

Piece of slate, 7 x 9 inches (17.8 x 22.9 cm), for the base of the vase

Smaller stones, various shapes and sizes

Pebbles and/or polished river rock

Instructions

1 Put the metal frog slightly off center in the cup, and glue it in place. Lay the larger pond stones down onto the slate, arranging them around the cupped frog to anchor it in place. Glue the bottom of the cup onto the slate, then adhere the stones. Use generous amounts of glue for a solid bond. Allow the glue to set for several hours.

2 Place the smaller stones around the cup, gluing them down one at a time and building the stack slowly.

3 Use several of the small, flat stones around the rim of the cup to create a ledge around the frog and to hide the cup. Leave as much open area as possible around the frog.

4 Fill in any gaps with small pebbles and river stones. Allow the adhesive to set for at least 24 hours before using the vase.

Faux Silver Leaf

Designers: Allison Smith and Terry Taylor

Designers Allison and Terry found a quick and easy way to get the look of silver leaf onto a glass vase.

Materials & Tools

Flared-body vase, 15 inches (38.1 cm)

Aluminum foil tape

Leaf-shape punch

Instructions

1 With the aluminum foil tape facing up, punch 30 leaves from the foil using the leaf-shape punch.

2 Turn the foil over and punch out 30 more leaves. This way you will have leaves that face two different directions.

3 Carefully remove the backing from the foil leaves, and place them onto the vase in a Grecian-style olive branch pattern.

4 Cut one 16-inch (40.6-cm) length of the foil tape. Trim two ¼-inch-wide (6-mm) strips from this length of tape.

5 Remove the backing and attach one of the strips of foil tape just above the top of the leaf pattern and the other one just below the bottom of the leaf pattern.

Toile Tin

Designer: Terry Taylor

Fanciful crimped-metal shapes, cut from a patterned cookie tin (a garage sale find), wake up this ho-hum container. A great look for a patio or sunroom.

Materials & Tools

Galvanized metal vase

Patterned cookie tin

Can opener

Protective gloves

Metal shears

Metal file

Nylon scrubbing pad

Scissors

Rubber cement

Ruler

Awl

Tack

Wood block

Round-nose pliers

Pop-rivet tool

Rivets

Instructions

1 Remove the bottom of the tin with the can opener. Wear protective gloves, and use the metal shears to cut along the seam of the tin. Remove the rolled edges of the tin with the metal shears, and flatten out the sheet of tin, pressing it with your hands. From the plain side of the metal, file the cut edges smooth, then give them a final finish with the scrubbing pad.

2 Draw an oval shape on a piece of paper. Cut out the design with scissors. Use the rubber cement to adhere the design to the undecorated side of the tin, and cut it out with the shears. Make a second shape in the same way.

3 Measure and cut two ⅝ x 16-inch (1.6 x 40.6-cm) strips of tin. These will be the bow loops.

4 Use the awl to pierce a small hole in the center of each strip. Trim a small hourglass shape, to make the bow shape, from each strip with the shears. Round the sharp corners at either end, then pierce a hole at each one.

5 Place the tack in the center hole of a strip. Bring the ends around and behind the tack, then tack the bow shape to the wood block. Crimp the bow shape with the round-nose pliers. Remove the tack. Set the bow to the side. Make a second bow shape with the other strip.

6 Measure and cut two ⅝ x 9-inch (1.6 x 22.9 cm) strips. Cut a notch in each end. For the tail of the bow, fold a 9-inch (22.9 cm) strip at an angle. Pierce a hole in the center at the fold. Crimp the strips with the round-nose pliers. Repeat for the other strip.

7 To receive the pop rivet, enlarge the holes on both the bow and on the angled strip. Pierce a hole on the vase. Assemble the bow and strip together. Rivet the ribbon bow to the vase.

8 Pierce two or more holes around the outer edge of the cut-out oval shape. Enlarge those holes to receive a pop rivet. Place one oval shape on the vase, and mark the position of the holes onto it. Enlarge one of the marked holes on the vase and rivet the design to the vase before riveting the others. Repeat this process for the second oval.

Equisetum Columns

Designer: Terry Taylor

Delicate dried *equisetum* (commonly known as "horsetail") makes a graphic statement when paired with handmade paper.

Materials & Tools

Glass cylinder vase

Decorative paper

Scissors

Hot-glue gun and glue sticks

Dried equisetum stems

Sharp craft knife

Instructions

1 Cut the paper to the height you need for the vase.

2 Wrap the paper around the vase, and cut it to the proper length, adding enough for a small overlap.

3 Hot glue the paper to the vase.

4 Trim the *equisetum* stems to the height of the vase with the craft knife.

5 Hot glue the stems to the paper.

Frosted Resin

Designer: Terry Taylor

No rule says that sleek and modern can't be beaded. This vase is adorned simply with large, resin beads that pack a powerful pink punch.

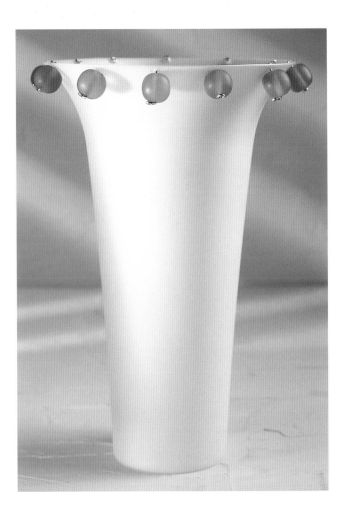

Materials & Tools

Resin vase

Awl

Wire cutter

20-gauge wire

Round-nose pliers

Resin beads

Instructions

1 Make evenly spaced marks on the rim of the vase with a pencil.

2 Turn the vase over and pierce each mark with the awl.

3 Use the wire cutter to cut the wire into the same number of 3-inch (7.6 cm) lengths as the number of holes you made in the vase.

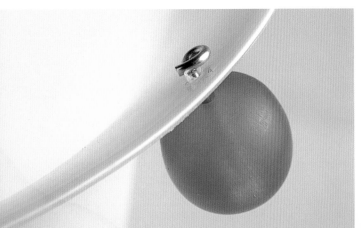

4 Use the round-nose pliers to make a small spiral in one end of a piece of wire. Thread one of the beads onto the wire. Fit the spiral snugly against the bead, making sure that the bead won't slip off.

5 Thread the wire through one of the pierced holes. Pull the bead tight against the vase, and wind a small spiral at the other end of the wire to hold it in place. Trim the wire.

6 Repeat steps 4 and 5 until you have put beads in each of the holes.

Fossil-Style Ikebana

Designer: Lynn B. Krucke

This polymer clay container evokes an idealized mountain landscape, in the Japanese tradition.

Materials & Tools

3 ounces (84 g) white polymer clay

Rolling pin or pasta machine dedicated to use with clay

Craft knife

Wax paper

Template, photocopied at 200%

Leaves, freshly picked

Coarse sandpaper or nylon scouring pad

Biscuit cutter or circle template, 1¼ inches (3.2 cm) in diameter

Glass tealight or votive candleholder, 1 inch (2.5 cm) in diameter

Baking tray

Ceramic tile

Acrylic paint, burnt umber

Paintbrush

Cotton rag

Waterproof glue

Metal needle holder type frog, 1 inch (2.5 cm) in diameter

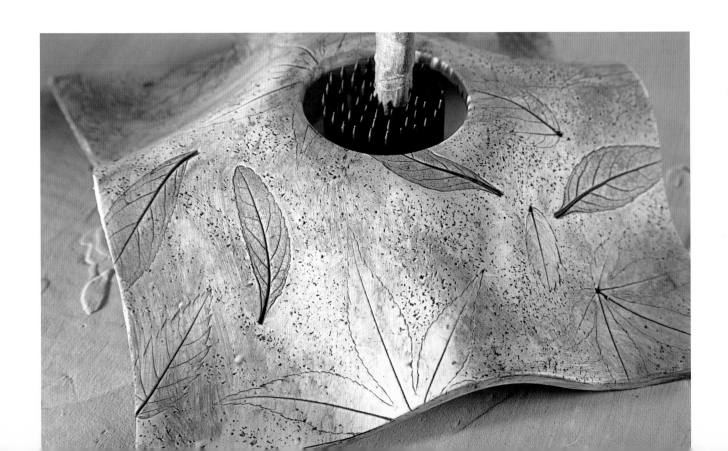

Instructions

1 Roll and knead the clay until it's soft and flexible. If you have a pasta machine, run the clay through it several times on the thickest setting. Fold the clay in half between each pass through the rollers with the folded edge inserted first. Roll out a sheet of clay ⅛ inch (3 mm) thick. Trim it with the craft knife so that it's slightly larger than the template. Place the sheet of clay onto a piece of wax paper.

2 Spread the leaves face up over the surface of the clay, and cover them with another piece of wax paper. Firmly press the leaves into the clay with the rolling pin or with your fingers. Remove the wax paper and texture the exposed areas of clay by patting them firmly with the sandpaper or scrubbing pad. Use the tip of the craft knife to carefully remove the leaves.

3 Place the template on the surface of the clay and cut around it. Remove the template.

4 With the biscuit cutter, make a hole at the center of the clay shape. Place the candleholder, bottom-side-up, on the baking tray. Remove the clay from the wax paper and drape the opening in the clay over the candleholder. You can adjust the clay's position, but it will shape itself during the baking. Place the ceramic tile facedown on the opening in the clay to keep it flat against the candleholder during baking. Bake the clay according to the manufacturer's instructions.

5 Once the clay is cool, paint it with a liberal amount of burnt umber acrylic paint. Wipe away the excess with the cotton rag while it's still wet, leaving paint in the impressions made by the leaves. Let the paint dry.

6 Use waterproof glue to glue the candleholder to the clay. Adhere the metal frog inside the vase.

Rusty Foliage

Designer: Terry Taylor

Materials & Tools

Metal container

Template, photocopied proportionate to container

Rusted craft tin

Rubber cement

Scissors

Cyanoacrylate glue

Instructions

1 Draw a leafy branch or photocopy the template several times.

2 Glue the patterns to the rusted tin with the rubber cement.

3 Cut out the shapes with the scissors.

4 Gently curve the shapes to the curve of the container.

5 Attach the shapes to the container with small dots of the cyanoacrylate glue.

Plain outdoor planters come alive in a flash with light-weight tin leaf shapes. Plant them with spring grass until the acorns fall.

Designer: Jean Tomaso Moore

Galvanized French Wrap

Bring the style of a French flower market home. Jean Tomaso Moore used natural materials as a rim embellishment on a flared metal pail.

Materials & Tools

Galvanized metal vase

1-inch-wide (2.5-cm) roll of masking tape

Flexible measuring tape

Safety glasses

Electric drill with ⅛-inch (3 mm) bit

Block of wood

Metal file

Rag

Metal primer spray paint

Black, high-gloss multi-purpose spray paint

Raffia (or similar natural weaving material)

Scissors

Instructions

1 Wrap the masking tape around the outside top rim of the container. Mark the bottom edge of the masking tape with a pencil at 1-inch (2.5 cm) intervals, using the flexible measuring tape as a guide.

2 Lay the container on its side on your work table. Put on safety glasses. Firmly hold the block of wood against the inside top rim of the vase. (This gives you something to brace against as you apply pressure with the drill.) Drill a ⅛ inch (3 mm) hole through the container (and into the wood) at each pencil mark. Remove the masking tape.

3 Use the metal file to smooth any rough spots around the drilled areas. Wipe down the container with the rag to remove any lingering metal debris.

4 Spray the outside of the container with one coat of primer, and let dry. Apply two coats of black paint over the primed container, allowing it to dry between coats.

5 From the inside of the vase, push two or three strands of raffia through one of the holes to the outside of the vase, leaving a short tail behind to use for tying off when you've completed wrapping the rim. Pull the raffia up and over the rim to the inside of the vase, then push it through the next hole to the outside of the vase. Repeat this weaving pattern through all of the holes around the rim.

6 When you've wrapped the entire rim, tie the beginning and end pieces of the raffia together with a knot, inside the vase, to secure the raffia in place. Snip off any excess raffia below the knot.

Entwined

Designer: Diana Light

Designer Diana Light made the most of an exciting oval ceramic vase with her stylish tone-on-tone embellishment.

Materials & Tools

Masking tape

45 feet (13.6 m) of cotton cord, ⅛ inch (3 mm) in diameter

Scissors

Craft glue

Oval ceramic vase, 10 inches (25.4 cm) tall

Cyanoacrylate glue

Instructions

1 Wrap masking tape at the point where you want to cut the cord, and then cut through it. This will keep the end of the cord from raveling. Put a few drops of craft glue on the end fibers. Let it dry, then peel off the tape.

2 Attach the glued end of the cord to the base of the vase with cyanoacrylate glue. Let it dry.

3 Wind the cord around and up the sides of the vase, attaching it with craft glue. Let the cord lay loosely enough so it isn't pulling or twisting on itself.

4 When the cord is at the desired height, tape and glue the end as you did in step 1. Glue it to the vase and let dry.

Postmodern Empire

This imperial red footed vase would have looked très chic in the Empress Josephine's salon or on Napoleon's portable camp desk.

Materials & Tools

Trumpet-shape metal vase

Self-adhesive shelf liner

Scissors

Red spray paint

Paint pen

Drill and drill bit

4 metal drawer knobs*

Screws

4 rubber washers

*The knobs come with screws, but you'll need to purchase shorter screws that still fit the knobs.

Instructions

1 Cut leaf shapes from the shelf paper. Place them on the vase as desired.

2 Spray paint the vase and let it dry. Give the vase a second coat of paint. Let it dry.

3 Remove the leaf stencils.

4 Use the paint pen to outline the leaf shapes.

5 Turn the vase upside down. Drill four holes in the bottom of the vase, spaced evenly from each corner.

6 Replace the screws for the metal drawer knobs with the shorter ones. Place a knob on the bottom of the vase, then place a small rubber washer on the screw before you tighten it.

Boxy Pix

Designer: Jean Tomaso Moore

Jean used the simplest materials to create this stunning high-contrast constructed vase. (Can you tell that it started out as a humble box?)

Materials & Tools

Rectangular or square container with flat sides wide enough to accommodate several columns of toothpick grids [this container measures 7 x 11 x 3 inches (17.8 x 27.9 x 7.6 cm)]

Sheet of black, handmade paper, large enough to cover the container

Scissors

Paintbrush

Water-base, clear-drying glue

500 round wooden toothpicks, 2¾ inches (7 cm) long

80 flat wooden toothpicks, 2¼ inches (5.7 cm) long

Water-base découpage medium (optional)

Instructions

1 Lay the container down on the handmade paper. Wrap the paper around the container, and cut away the excess, leaving 1 inch (2.5 cm) at the top and bottom to overlap the edges.

2 Spread the glue over one side of the container with the paintbrush. Lay the paper down on the glued surface, leaving some overlap at the top and bottom. Smooth out the paper to remove any wrinkles or air bubbles. Cover each side of the container one side at a time.

3 Place a bead of glue along the top inner rim and along the bottom edge. Smooth down the overlaps onto the glue. Let the paper dry.

4 Stand the container up on a piece of the paper. Apply glue to the bottom of the container, and press it onto the paper. Smooth the paper across the bottom. Cut away the excess paper from around the base with the scissors.

5 Cut a 4-inch (10.2-cm) band of paper long enough to wrap around the entire container. This piece will be attached to the inside top rim of the container to help blend the interior with the exterior background. Apply glue to the paper band, gently place it along the top inner rim of the container, and smooth out the wrinkles. Let the paper dry thoroughly.

6 Place the container flat on a work surface with one long side facing you. Copy the grid pattern of the toothpicks shown here, or devise one of your own. Unless you find a container of the same dimensions as mine, you should work out the spacing of the toothpicks before you begin gluing them down in the next step.

7 Starting at the top left corner, use the paintbrush to spread a 3- to 4-inch (7.6- to 10.2-cm) square of glue onto the papered surface. Apply toothpicks horizontally on the glue, leaving small spaces between each one. Continue alternating the directions of the blocks of toothpicks until the entire surface is covered. (The container was too narrow to accommodate the longer, round toothpicks in both directions, so I alternated them with flat toothpicks.) Continue the process for the rest of the container.

8 If you want, apply a coat of découpage medium to protect the surface. Let it dry thoroughly.

Silver-Leaf Pinstripe

Designer: Jean Tomaso Moore

Paint softly glowing stripes onto a flat-sided ceramic vase. Perfect for a bedside table or breakfast tray!

Materials & Tools

Small three-sided ceramic vase

Ruler

Striping tape, ⅛ inch (3 mm) wide (available from auto supply stores)

Scissors

Liquid silver leaf

Disposable paintbrush

Instructions

1 Measure and mark the center point on each side of the vase with the pencil. Lay a piece of striping tape along the center of one side of the vase. Firmly press the tape in place. Repeat for the remaining two sides of the vase.

2 Working on one side of the vase at a time, cut two 1-inch-long (2.5-cm) strips of tape and butt them up against each side of the first strip you applied. (These pieces will act as spacers and guides for placing the longer tape strips at equal distances from one another.) Lay a full-length strip alongside each spacer. Continue alternating spacers with full-length strips until that side of the vase is filled. Repeat the taping pattern for the other sides, working outward from the center.

3 Remove all the spacers. Paint a coat of liquid leaf onto the exposed parts of the vase. Allow the first coat to dry, then apply a second coat. When the paint is thoroughly dry, carefully remove the tape.

Folk Art

Designer: Jean Tomaso Moore

Designer Jean Tomaso Moore brought all the elements of a folk-art theme to this planter-style vase with soft colors and simple shapes on wood.

Materials & Tools

4-sided wooden container, 5½ x 6 inches
(14 x 15.2 cm)

Acrylic craft paint in brown (for base coat),
white, aqua, light turquoise, several shades of
green, black, yellow, orange, and pink, 2 ounces
(60 ml) each

Assorted paintbrushes

Foam plate or shallow bowl for holding paint

Paper towels or rags

Carbon paper or transfer paper

4 pieces of lightweight craft wood, each
3 inches (7.6 cm) square

120-grit sandpaper

Scissors

Black fine-point permanent marker

Ruler

Wood glue

Matte acrylic spray varnish

Instructions

1 Use a large paintbrush to apply an overall base
coat of brown paint to it. Allow the paint to dry.

2 Use a dry paintbrush to achieve a light, dry
application of aqua paint over the brown coat.
Wipe away some of the paint with a paper towel
to let the brown stain show through. Allow the
paint to dry, then apply the light turquoise paint in
the same way.

3 Mix a small amount of white paint with water
in your paint palette to create a wash solution.
Coat the entire container with the whitewash,
allowing it to seep into crevices and into the wood
grain. Let the container sit for several minutes,
then wipe away the excess wash with a paper
towel. Repeat this last step until you've achieved
the desired distressed finish.

4 Lightly sand the edges and corners of the
squares to soften them. Wipe away any wood
debris with a rag. Apply white paint as a base coat
to one side of each square, and let dry.

5 Draw a simple motif onto paper (or you might
want to use four different designs for each of the
four sides of the container). Sandwich the carbon or
transfer paper between the design and the painted
side of the square. Use the pencil to trace over the
design, transferring the pattern to the wood.

6 Use the permanent marker to outline the
design on a wood square, then fill it in with assorted colors of craft paint. Repeat steps 5 and 6 for
the other squares if you want designs on them.

7 Measure and mark the center of each side of
the container. Spread glue on the back of a square,
center it over the mark you made, and press it in
place. Glue the rest of the squares to the container
in the same manner.

8 When the glue has dried, spray one or two
coats of matte acrylic varnish over the container's
surfaces to seal and protect your artwork.

Fluted Brass

Designer: Joan K. Morris

The designer gussied up an ordinary clear-glass vase with her clever pleated "sleeve" creation.

Materials & Tools

Flared-body glass vase with narrow neck, 7 inches (17.8 cm) tall

Brass screen mesh, cut to a 9 x 20-inch (22.9 x 50.8 cm) rectangle

Ice pick or hole punch

Brass wire

Hot-glue gun with glue sticks

Thin gold cording, 4 feet (1.22 m) long

2 glass beads

Instructions

1 Make ½-inch (1.3 cm) accordions in the piece of brass screen along the 9-inch (22.9-cm) end.

2 Carefully stretch the middle of the pleats around the widest part of the vase. Where the edges meet, punch holes through them.

3 Weave the brass wire through the holes to close the edges.

4 At the bottom of the vase, overlap the pleats so that the screen fits the vase well, and hot glue them into place.

5 At the narrowest part of the neck, punch a hole through each folded pleat.

6 Cut 24 inches (61 cm) of cording and pass it through the holes in the neck, with one end of the cord 1 inch (2.5 cm) longer than the other. Pull the lacing tight, and tie a knot in it.

7 Thread the glass beads onto the ends of the cord, and tie knots below them.

8 With the remaining 24 inches (61 cm) of the cord, wrap it three times around the bottom of the vase, and tie it in back. Hot glue it into place.

Tuscan Revival

Designer: Terry Taylor

Designer Terry made this witty vase, based on a classic urn profile, from a couple of olive oil cans.

Materials & Tools

2 large olive oil cans (you can find empty ones at a local restaurant)

Can opener

Protective gloves

Tin snips

Paper

Pencil

Rubber cement

Metal file

Nylon kitchen scrubber

Wood dowel, 1 inch (2.5 cm) in diameter

Awl

Pop-rivet tool and rivets

Instructions

1 Remove the top of one can with the can opener. Remove both the top and bottom of the second can. Thoroughly wash and dry both cans.

2 Wearing protective gloves, use the tin snips to cut along the seam of the bottomless can. Flatten it with your hands on a smooth surface.

3 Draw a 2-inch-wide (5 cm) rectangle on a piece of paper that is 1½ times as long as the can is tall. Within the confines of the rectangle, sketch a symmetrical shape for a handle.

4 Glue the paper shape to the flattened can with the rubber cement, then cut it out with the shears. Re-glue the pattern to another part of the can, and cut a second handle shape.

5 File the edges of the cut shapes with the file. Use the kitchen scrubber to give a final finish to the edges.

6 Curve the handle shapes as desired. Shape them on the wood dowel to maintain a uniform curve. Make them as symmetrical as you can.

7 Pierce the top of one handle with the awl. Enlarge the hole as needed to fit the rivet.

8 Place the shaped handle on the can. Mark where the hole on the handle meets the can, and then pierce the can with the awl.

9 Use the pop rivet tool to set the rivet. Pierce the bottom of the handle, and rivet it into place. Repeat on the opposite side of the can.

Textured Gold

Designer: Joan K. Morris

Get as textured as you like with the gold-foil treatment.
It's fancy enough to use as a dinner table centerpiece.

Materials & Tools

Curvy glass vase, 9 inches (22.9 cm) tall

Dimensional acrylic adhesive

Burgundy paint

Paintbrush

Gold foil

Gold foil adhesive

Black paint

Small bucket

Rag

Polyurethane clear satin spray

Instructions

1 Following the manufacturer's instructions, draw designs onto the surface of the vase with the dimensional glue. Let the adhesive dry thoroughly.

2 Paint the outside of the vase with burgundy paint. Let it dry.

3 Following the manufacturer's instructions, glue the gold foil to the vase with the gold foil adhesive. Cover the burgundy paint and about 1 inch (2.5 cm) of the inside neck of the vase.

4 Let the vase dry completely.

5 Dilute the black paint by mixing equal parts water and paint in the bucket. Paint the mixture over the gold foil, then immediately wipe it off with the rag. Let it dry. Now the vase has a burnished, antique look.

6 Spray several coats of the polyurethane over the vase, letting it dry between coats.

Celtic Etch

Designer: Diana Light

Designer Diana Light gave an ancient Celtic-knot motif some ultramodern flair on this Scandinavian glass vase.

Materials & Tools

Smoked-glass oval vase

Self-adhesive shelf liner

Scissors

Small squeegee

Tape

Carbon paper

Template, photocopied at 100%

Swivel-blade craft knife

Straight-blade craft knife

Cotton swabs

Etching cream

Instructions

1 Clean and dry the vase. Cut a piece of shelf liner to cover the front of the vase plus a 2-inch (5-cm) border on all sides.

2 Peel off the backing, lay the shelf liner onto the glass, and smooth out the air bubbles with the squeegee. Save the backing piece.

3 Tape a piece of carbon paper the size of the template onto the liner. Center and tape the template on top of it. Use a pencil to transfer the design onto the liner. This will be your stencil.

4 Remove the template and the carbon paper. Carefully cut on all the lines with the swivel-blade knife.

5 Use the straight-edge craft knife to pull the liner out of the negative spaces of the design. To be sure the liner is in firm contact with the glass, lay the backing paper you saved over the stencil and pull the squeegee across the stencil. Use cotton swabs, slightly moistened with water, to wipe off any adhesive that may have gotten onto the areas that will be etched.

6 Stir the etching cream well. With one hand supporting the 2-inch (5 cm) border on one side, pour the cream onto the liner. Use the squeegee to pull the cream evenly and quickly across the design. Leave the cream on the vase for the amount of time recommended by the etching cream manufacturer.

7 Wash off the cream under running water, being careful not to smear cream anywhere else on the vase. Remove the adhesive liner, and dry the vase.

Debba Haupert lives in Cincinnati, Ohio, with her pets and her supportive (and creative!) husband. She provides support services to the hobby and craft industry through her company, BoBella Craft Marketing & Design LLC. She has designed craft projects for television, books, magazines and manufacturers. Visit her website at www.bobella.com.

Lynn Krucke is an instructor and a designer who works with many different types of media, including rubber stamps and paper arts, polymer clay, beads and wire, and fabric/fiber arts. Her designs have been included in many craft books, and she's appeared on the nationally syndicated television program *The Carol Duvall Show*. Lynn lives in Summerville, South Carolina. Contact Lynn at lkrucke@bellsouth.net.

Diana Light is a D. Light-ful artist who has an uncanny ability to make everything she touches look absolutely fabulous and instantly cool. After earning her B.F.A. in painting and printmaking, Diana extended her expertise to etching and painting fine glass objects. She has contributed to numerous Lark books and lives and works in the beautiful Blue Ridge Mountains of North Carolina.

Jill MacKay is a versatile, self-taught artist, craftsperson, designer, and parent. A wide range of life experience and knowledge of the natural world and of human nature create the basis and inspiration for her work. Jill also is a nationally recognized community artist. She lives in Pittsburgh, Pennsylvania, with her two teenage children, and works out of her studio at home.

Livia McRee is an avid craft writer and a designer. Born in Nashville, Tennessee, and raised in New York City by her artist parents, Livia always has been captivated by and immersed in folk and fine arts as well as in graphic design. She's the author of three books, and her work can be found in many craft publications. Visit her website at www.liviamcree.com.

Jean Tomaso Moore is a part-time multimedia artist who has been creating art in one form or another for as long as she can remember. She lives with her humble and patient husband in Asheville, North Carolina.

Joan K. Morris' artistic endeavors have led her down many successful creative paths. A childhood interest in sewing turned into a career in professional costuming for motion pictures. After studying ceramics, Joan ran her own clay wind chime business. Since 1993, Joan's Asheville, North Carolina, coffee house, Vincent's Ear, has provided a vital meeting place for all varieties of artists and thinkers. Joan's craft projects have been featured in a number of Lark books.

Robin Schoenfeld began her professional life as a registered nurse, so the more creative direction she has ended up taking is as much a surprise to her as it is to everyone else. She lives and works very enthusiastically in mixed media in Tarzana, California, with her wonderfully tolerant husband, two handsome sons, and several liberally paint-spattered cats and dogs.

Allison Smith lives in Asheville, North Carolina. Her home-based business specializes in providing deluxe tourist accommodations in remote locations in Western North Carolina. She's an avid crafter and a designer as well as a full-time mother. She has created projects for numerous Lark books, including: *Decorating Baskets*, *Girls' World*, and *Decorating Candles*.

Terry B. Taylor has the coolest pair of bright red shoes a person could ever hope to own. In addition to footwear flair, he is an extremely (some would say unfairly) talented artist and self-styled craft maven. His work has been featured in books, galleries, and on television. Thankfully, the fame and fortune he received from his first appearance on *The Christopher Lowell Show* did not go to his head.

Acknowledgments

This book is much the better for the gracious last-minute help of Linda Arbuckle, Elizabeth (Libby) Campbell, and Ronni Lundy; thanks also to the outstanding support team of Rain Newcomb, Anne Hollyfield, and Veronika Alice Gunter, whose amazing attention to detail, good humor, and many helpful acts made the book not only possible, but the richer for their contributions; finally, a big, crooked happy smile to the dynamic duo of professional photography team Keith and Wendy Wright, who brought art director Tom Metcalf's confident artistic vision to fruition.

Index